YOU CHO

CAN YOU SURVIVE the Johnstown FLOOD?

AN INTERACTIVE HISTORY ADVENTURE

by Steven Otfinoski

CAPSTONE PRESS
a capstone imprint

Published by Capstone Press, an imprint of Capstone.
1710 Roe Crest Drive
North Mankato, Minnesota 56003
capstonepub.com

Copyright © 2022 by Capstone. All rights reserved. No part of this publication may be reproduced in whole or in part, or stored in a retrieval system, or transmitted in any form or by any means, electronic, mechanical, photocopying, recording, or otherwise, without written permission of the publisher.

Library of Congress Cataloging-in-Publication Data
Names: Otfinoski, Steven, author.
Title: Can you survive the Johnstown flood? : an interactive history adventure / Steven Otfinoski.
Description: North Mankato, Minnesota : Capstone Press, an imprint of Capstone, [2022] | Series: You choose: disasters in history | Includes bibliographical references and index. | Audience: Ages 8-12. | Audience: Grades 4-6. | Summary: "On May 31, 1889, heavy rains and a dam failure sent flood waters sweeping into Johnstown, Pennsylvania. The 50-foot-high wall of water quickly demolished much of the town. Will you and your new husband be able to escape certain doom as you wait for your train to leave the station? Can you climb onto your house's roof for safety before the building completely fills with water? Will you join in the effort to save others who are floating by on the roofs of their houses? With dozens of possible choices, it's up to YOU to find a way to survive one of the deadliest disasters in American history"-- Provided by publisher.
Identifiers: LCCN 2021033282 (print) | LCCN 2021033283 (ebook) | ISBN 9781663958952 (hardcover) | ISBN 9781666323641 (paperback) | ISBN 9781666323658 (ebook pdf)
Subjects: LCSH: Floods--Pennsylvania--Johnstown (Cambria County)--History--19th century--Juvenile literature. | Dam failures--Pennsylvania--Johnstown (Cambria County)--History--19th century--Juvenile literature. | Survival--Juvenile literature. | Johnstown (Cambria County, Pa.)--History--19th century--Juvenile literature.
Classification: LCC F159.J7 O84 2022 (print) | LCC F159.J7 (ebook) | DDC 974.8/7704--dc23
LC record available at https://lccn.loc.gov/2021033282
LC ebook record available at https://lccn.loc.gov/2021033283

Editorial Credits
Editor: Aaron Sautter; Designer: Bobbie Nuytten; Media Researcher: Morgan Walters; Production Specialist: Laura Manthe

All internet sites appearing in back matter were available and accurate when this book was sent to press.

Printed and bound in China. 5378

TABLE OF CONTENTS

About Your Adventure 5

CHAPTER 1
An Unnatural Disaster 7

CHAPTER 2
A Honeymoon Interrupted 13

CHAPTER 3
The Girl on the Mattress 41

CHAPTER 4
A Clerk to the Rescue 71

CHAPTER 5
A Tragedy's Long Shadow 101

Johnstown Flood Timeline 106
Other Paths to Explore 108
Bibliography 109
Glossary 110
Read More 111
Internet Sites 111
About the Author 112

ABOUT YOUR ADVENTURE

YOU are living in Johnstown, Pennsylvania, in 1889. One day at the end of May, heavy rains fall on the area, causing a nearby dam to burst. Within minutes, a huge wall of water rushes through town, washing away everything in its path. Will you be able to get out of the way before the flood sweeps you away too?

Chapter One sets the scene. Then you choose which path to read. Follow the directions at the bottom of the page as you read the stories. The decisions you make will change your outcome. After you finish one path, go back and read the others for new perspectives and more adventures.

Turn the page to begin your adventure.

After the South Fork dam collapsed, flood waters from Lake Conemaugh hit the towns of Mineral Point, East Conemaugh, and Woodvale before destroying Johnstown.

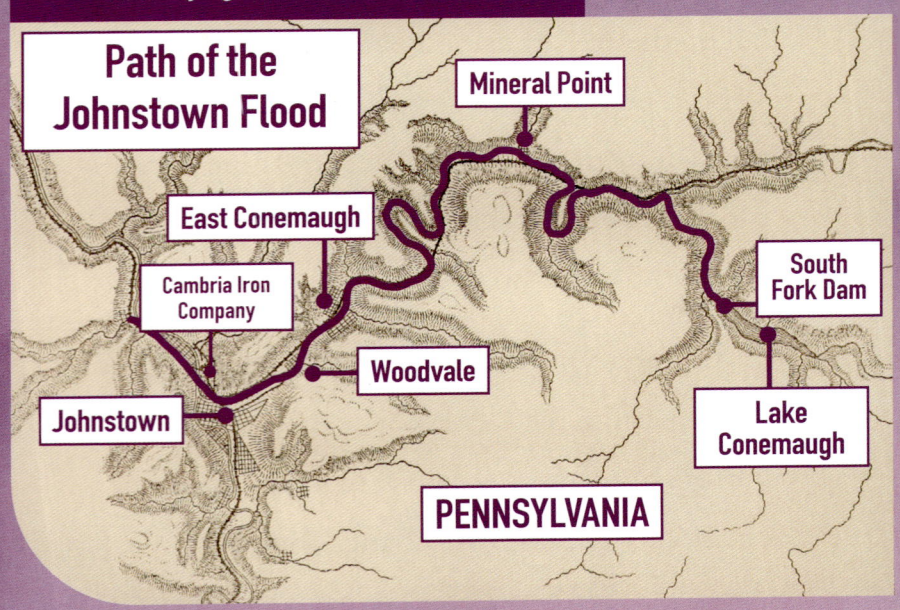

Path of the Johnstown Flood

CHAPTER 1
AN UNNATURAL DISASTER

Natural disasters are often unavoidable. But some past disasters could have been prevented and lives and property spared. What happened in Johnstown, Pennsylvania, on May 31, 1889, was one such "unnatural" disaster. It was the result of neglect and greed rather than the powerful forces of nature.

The roots of this tragedy started nearly 50 years earlier. In the 1840s the state of Pennsylvania built an earthen dam across the Conemaugh River. The resulting reservoir supplied water for a recently built railroad and canal system between the cities of Philadelphia and Pittsburgh.

Turn the page.

The city of Johnstown lay just 14 miles (23 kilometers) downriver from the dam. Johnstown was the home of the Cambria Iron Company, which before the Civil War (1861–65) was the biggest ironworks in America.

In 1857 the state sold the dam and reservoir to the Pennsylvania Railroad. The dam steadily declined over time, and repairs made by the railroad were inadequate.

In 1879 millionaire Benjamin Ruff bought the property. He turned it into a summer resort for the industry owners of Pittsburgh. He named it the South Fork Fishing and Hunting Club. The founding members included wealthy men such as Andrew Carnegie, Henry C. Frick, and Andrew Mellon. The club rebuilt the existing dam, creating a larger lake where the reservoir had stood.

The new Lake Conemaugh was used by club members and their families for boating, fishing, and swimming. However, the club members did little to maintain the dam. Over time, it continued to deteriorate.

A few people in Johnstown saw the dam as a danger. Daniel J. Morrell, president of the Cambria Iron Company, insisted that the dam needed to be restructured. He even offered to do the job himself. But the club members showed little concern.

Morrell died in 1885. That same year, the area saw heavy spring rains and flooding on the Conemaugh River. Flooding returned in 1887 and 1888. But the people of Johnstown were used to spring floods and accepted them as a part of life.

Turn the page.

Thursday, May 30, 1889, was Decoration Day, which today is known as Memorial Day. The city was in a happy mood "with flags, banners and flowers everywhere," recalled one of the city's ministers.

Rain begins to fall that afternoon and continues through the night. At dawn on May 31, 23-year-old John Parke, an engineer at the South Fork Club, is measuring the water at the dam. He finds that it has risen 2 feet (0.6 meter). He realizes that if the water reaches the top of the dam, the structure will crumble and burst. But there's little he can do to stop it.

By late morning, Johnstown's streets are flooded from the heavy rains. But people aren't panicking. They're used to moving furniture to the second floor of their homes and businesses to prevent water damage.

At 3:10 p.m. the dam at South Fork bursts. At least 20 million tons of water from Lake Conemaugh rushes down the valley in a 40-foot (12-m) wave of destruction.

Three small communities are in the flood's path before it will hit Johnstown. At Mineral Point, nearly every home is washed away by the flood. East Conemaugh is next. A train station is located there, and several passenger and freight trains sit in the station yard.

You're in the path of the flood and must find a way to survive. What are you going to do before the flood strikes?

To be a newlywed bride at the East Conemaugh train station, turn to page 13.

To be a young girl in Johnstown at home with your family, turn to page 41.

To be a salesclerk working at the Cambria Iron Company store, turn to page 71.

In the late 1800s, taking a train was the quickest way to travel between U.S. cities.

CHAPTER 2
A HONEYMOON INTERRUPTED

It is just after 3:00 p.m. on May 31, 1889. You and your new husband, John, are sitting on the Day Express train at the East Conemaugh station. The train can't move because the tracks have been washed out further down the line. Until they're repaired, you're stuck. You should be upset and angry, but you're not.

While other passengers wander around the tracks in the rain, you and John sit on the train, holding hands. You talk about all the wonderful things you'll do on your honeymoon in Philadelphia when you finally get there.

Turn the page.

Suddenly you hear the shrill shriek of a train whistle. You've heard train whistles before, but this one is extremely loud and continues endlessly. Then the conductor comes running into the car.

"Everyone off the train!" he cries. "Get to the hill!"

"What's happened?" John asks.

"The engineer says the dam at South Fork has burst!" he replies and runs into the next car.

You grab John's hand and follow the other passengers out into the pouring rain.

You see a throng of people rushing uphill to higher ground. You start after them but suddenly stop.

"My handbag. I left it on the seat," you say. "My grandmother's wedding ring is in it."

The ring is a precious family heirloom that is now your wedding ring. However, it's a little too small, and you took it off after the wedding. You planned to get it resized at a jeweler's shop in Philadelphia.

"I'll go back for it," says John. "It'll only take a minute."

To let John go back for your ring, turn to page 16.

To stop him and move uphill, turn to page 17.

John dashes back to the train. But as he enters the car, a towering wall of water descends on the station yard. It engulfs the train you were on and everything else in its path.

A man standing by seizes your hand. "You've got to run!" he cries. He pulls you forward uphill. You never see your dear John alive again. For the sake of a ring, you have lost the man you love.

THE END

To follow another path, turn to page 9.
To learn more about the flood, turn to page 101.

"Forget the ring," you tell John. "There's no time to waste."

Together, hand in hand, you run for the hillside. But an obstacle blocks your path. It's another train, four cars long.

You see a few people crawling under it to get to the other side. Others are scrambling up the side of the train and climbing over the top. Still others are running down the tracks to get around the train. What will you and John do? There's no time to lose!

> To run around the train, turn to page 18.
> To crawl under the train, turn to page 19.
> To climb over the train, turn to page 22.

You and John run down the length of the cars to get to the other side. Breathless, you make it around the last car, only to find another obstacle in your path.

It's a ditch about 10 feet (3 m) wide, half-filled with rainwater. It's too wide to jump over. You turn and see a long wooden plank by the ditch. Maybe it's long enough to use as a bridge across the ditch. The two of you grasp the plank, but it's too heavy to lift by yourselves.

"Need a hand with that?" speaks a deep voice. You turn and see a husky man with a beard as black as coal standing nearby.

Turn to page 21.

You and John get down on your hands and knees and begin to crawl under the train. But as you're crawling along, your dress gets snagged on a spike sticking up from the track.

As you struggle to free the dress, you look up to see a wall of water descend on the station yard. It slams into the train. The huge wheels roll forward, crushing both you and John. Your honeymoon—and your lives—come to an unexpected end.

THE END

To follow another path, turn to page 9.
To learn more about the flood, turn to page 101.

People at the East Conemaugh train station had little warning before the floodwaters hit.

"We sure could!" replies John. The man grabs one end of the plank while you and John lift the other. You quickly make your way to the ditch and drop the plank across it. It barely reaches the other side.

But before you can cross over the plank, other people come running in a panic. Once the crowd has passed, you, John, and your new friend run onto the plank.

CRACK!

Just as you reach the other side of the ditch, you hear the plank break. The big man with the beard was behind you. The plank has broken in two, and he's fallen into the ditch. You see his head bobbing in the dark waters, and his arms are splashing helplessly.

Turn to page 27.

You used to climb trees as a kid and have little trouble climbing to the roof of the train car. Then you help pull John up to join you. Side by side, you stand atop the train and look north. You see a wall of water rushing toward you. There's no time to climb down.

"We've got to jump for it!" cries John. Hand in hand, you leap to the muddy ground below.

You both hit the wet earth hard. You land on your feet and feel a sharp pain in your right ankle. There's no time to see if it's broken. You start to move forward, but the pain in your ankle is intense.

"Let me carry you," says John.

You hesitate as he holds out his arms. Both of you might fall if he tries to carry you all the way up the hill. Maybe it's better if you lean your weight on him and hop on your one good leg.

> To let John carry you up the hill, turn to page 25.
>
> To lean on your husband and hop up the hill, turn to page 26.

Those who made it to safety could only look on helplessly as the huge flood swept away buildings, trees, and unlucky victims.

You let John lift you into his arms. He starts up the hillside, struggling to carry you. The grass on the hill is wet and slick, and John begins to slip. Then he steadies himself and regains his footing. John is panting heavily now. He can't hold you much longer without stopping to rest. You can hear the awful roar of the wall of water.

With a final burst of speed, John rushes to the top of the hill. He lets you down gently on the wet grass. Then you stare down at the terrible scene below. Your train and several others are floating down the river like a child's toys, crashing and bashing into each other.

It looks like train service to Philadelphia won't resume anytime soon. But the two of you are alive, and that's all that matters.

THE END

To follow another path, turn to page 9.
To learn more about the flood, turn to page 101.

"Don't try to pick me up," you tell your husband. "I can walk if I lean on you."

John wraps one arm around your waist and pulls you up next to him. You lift your foot with the bad ankle and hop on your good leg. In a couple of minutes, you make it to the hilltop. You sit on the grass and watch as the flood sweeps away everything below, including wagons, broken roofs, large trees, and more.

"Where will the water go next?" you ask John.

"There's the small town of Woodvale below," he replies. "Then it'll be headed straight for Johnstown."

You shiver at the thought. "At least we had a warning from that engineer," you say. "Johnstown will have no warning."

The two of you pray silently for the people of Johnstown.

Turn to page 32.

As you look down at the helpless man in the muddy water, you know you can't leave him behind.

"John!" you cry. "We've got to help him."

John turns around and looks at the rushing waters. "I don't think there's time," he says.

Your heart sinks at the thought of leaving him.

To keep going, turn to page 28.

To try to rescue your newfound friend, turn to page 30.

Maybe John's right. There's no time to go back. He grabs your hand, and together you race up the slippery hillside. You finally reach the crest and collapse on the grass.

For a time, neither of you says a word. You know that John is probably feeling just as bad as you are about the man you left behind. Heavy raindrops are falling on your face, mixing with the tears running down your cheeks. You don't think you'll ever forget the man's face as he looked up at you from the ditch.

Then suddenly you hear someone crying close by.

You turn and see a young girl sitting nearby. She is sobbing loudly. You put an arm around her shivering body.

"I can't find my mother," she cries. "She told me to run up the hill, and now I can't find her."

"We'll wait here with you until she comes," you tell the girl, holding her tightly.

Turn to page 38.

Both people and animals acted heroically during the flood. Romey the dog, pictured here, saved three members of the Kress family that day.

You can't leave this man to die.

"John," you say, "we've got to help him."

John nods in agreement, and the two of you race back to the ditch. You grab the big man's arms and pull. It's a struggle, but you succeed in getting him out of the ditch.

You and John then throw an arm around his shoulders and guide him up the hillside. As you reach the top, the three of you collapse on the grass just as the floodwaters rush by below.

"Thank you," gasps the man. "I thought I was a goner. I guess I won't be getting to Philadelphia today."

"That's where we're going too," you say.

He looks at you and John in your nice clothes. "Oh?" he asks. "On vacation?"

"Honeymoon," you reply. "Although I don't know if we'll have much of one now."

"Nonsense!" replies the man. "Not even a flood should ruin such a happy occasion!"

Turn to page 35.

Although many escaped the flood, at least 22 people died when it destroyed this train in East Conemaugh.

You spend the next few days in East Conemaugh. You hear news of the devastation the flood has brought to Johnstown. Your ankle aches, and you rest in a small tent while John tries to find medical aid. But the only doctor in town is busy treating patients with more serious injuries.

You'll have to wait your turn to see the doctor. Or you could wait for the train service to be restored and find a doctor in Johnstown.

To see the doctor in East Conemaugh, go to page 33.

To take the train into Johnstown, turn to page 34.

You decide to wait for the local doctor. The next day he examines your ankle and recommends a crutch to help you walk. He's busy with other patients and offers no other care for your injury.

By the time you get to Philadelphia, your ankle is hurting worse than ever. You see a doctor there who wraps your ankle in a bandage. He says the muscle is badly torn and will require a long rest. Your honeymoon is a bust, and you'll be spending most of it in bed. Too bad!

THE END

To follow another path, turn to page 9.
To learn more about the flood, turn to page 101.

By week's end, train service is restored. You and John make the short trip into Johnstown.

Many residents are wandering the streets, still recovering from the loss of their homes and loved ones. But others, like you, are tourists and sightseers. As you stare at the few buildings still standing, you begin to realize the enormity of this tragedy.

You and John make your way to a large Red Cross tent. Inside the tent are rows of cots with injured people lying on them.

John explains to a passing doctor about your injured ankle. The doctor examines it.

"It doesn't seem to be fractured," he says. "Probably a torn muscle."

Turn to page 36.

The man explains that he is the owner of one of the biggest hotels in Philadelphia.

"You must stay at my hotel," he tells you. "In the honeymoon suite!"

"That's very kind of you. But we already have a reservation," John says. He tells the man about the hotel where you'll be staying.

"Not to worry," the man replies. "I know the owner there. We'll cancel the reservation. It won't be a problem."

Turn to page 39.

The doctor rubs some strong-smelling ointment on your ankle and then bandages it. "Try to stay off it as much as you can," he tells you. "You can rest here for a while if you wish."

You do exactly that as John leaves to find a room for the night.

A few minutes later, a short elderly woman in a black dress enters the tent. She smiles at you.

"How are you feeling, dear?" she asks.

You explain how you and John survived the flood in East Conemaugh and made your way to Johnstown.

"You're among the lucky ones," she says. "There are so many people here who need our help. But we'll stay until the job is done."

Then she moves on to check other patients in the tent. After she leaves, the doctor who helped you returns.

"Who was that little old woman in the black dress?" you ask. "Is she a nurse?"

The doctor laughs. "Heavens no," he says. "That was Clara Barton. She's the leader and founder of the American Red Cross. Without her, we wouldn't be here."

You recall hearing about this amazing woman, but you never thought you'd meet her face to face. John returns and tells you he's found a room for the night before you catch the morning train for Philadelphia.

"Well, it won't be much of a honeymoon now, will it?" you ask.

"Oh, I think we'll manage. Just don't expect to do any dancing," he says with a smile.

THE END

To follow another path, turn to page 9.
To learn more about the flood, turn to page 101.

You scan the faces of the men and women coming up the hill. Some carry small children in their arms.

"Carrie?" a thin, tall man asks.

"Uncle Amos!" cries the girl as she runs into his arms.

"This is your niece?" John asks.

"Yes, yes," he replies. "Thank you for staying with her. Her mother, my sister, lost track of her in the crowd."

This horrible day will end happily at least for this family, and you played a part in that. You are crying again—but now they're tears of joy.

THE END

To follow another path, turn to page 9.
To learn more about the flood, turn to page 101.

"Are you sure—" you begin to ask, but the man cuts you off.

"Don't be silly," he says. "I owe you my life, and I want to show a token of my appreciation. Just consider it my wedding present."

You can tell he is used to getting his way. It looks like your interrupted honeymoon will have a happy ending after all.

THE END

To follow another path, turn to page 9.
To learn more about the flood, turn to page 101.

The streets of Johnstown were already flooded from heavy rains that fell the night before the dam burst.

CHAPTER 3
THE GIRL ON THE MATTRESS

It is 3:45 p.m. on this rainy Friday afternoon. You're 10 years old and your father runs the biggest dry goods store in Johnstown. He's gone to the store to secure it from the flooding waters caused by the rain. The rain has turned your front yard into a pond. As you dangle your feet in the water, you watch some ducks paddling around.

Suddenly you see your father walking up the pathway to your house. His eyes flash when he sees you. *Uh-oh*, you think. He told you not to go outside. Now you're in for it!

Your father yanks you up to your feet and brings you inside. He tells you to put on clean, dry stockings and a dress.

Turn the page.

If your mother were home, she'd tell your father to calm down. But she's away visiting relatives. Your Aunt Abbie, who lives with you, is in charge. But she's not one to stand up to your father.

"As soon as she's dressed, we're going up the hill," your father says. "We'll be safe there."

For once, your aunt speaks back to your father. "Don't you think that's rash?" she asks. "The rain will stop soon."

"It's not the rain I'm worried about," says your father. "If the South Fork Dam bursts, it'll sweep away every house in town." Your father is one of the few men in Johnstown who has expressed concern about the dam. But no one has listened.

As he waits for you to get dressed, your father lights a cigar. A minute later he steps out the front door to knock the ash from the cigar. He steps back inside for a moment, his face pale as a sheet.

"Grab the children!" he tells your aunt urgently. "There's not a moment to lose."

Your father seizes the hands of your two younger sisters and starts out the door. Aunt Abbie and you follow close behind. You hear an unearthly roar from down the street and see a wall of water moving toward you. "Follow me!" your father cries.

But your aunt comes to an abrupt stop in the front yard. "The hill's too far," she murmurs. "We'll never make it. We'll be safer in the house."

She turns and runs for the front steps.

> To follow your aunt back to the house, turn to page 44.
>
> To run with your father to the hill, turn to page 46.

43

You follow your aunt back into the house and up the stairs to the third floor. You worry about your father, but you feel he'll make it to the hill. After all, he survived four years as a Union cavalry officer in the Civil War. You look out the front window and see people scrambling up Main Street, trying to keep ahead of the towering tide of water.

Aunt Abbie pulls you into a closet. She slams the door shut, engulfing you both in darkness.

CRACK!

A loud noise fills your ears. *Is it the walls of your house?* you wonder. You look down and see light coming through the floorboards. Then you hear a giant swoosh of rushing water.

As you stare at the floor in horror, the boards start to break up. Muddy water spurts up like a geyser. Aunt Abbie screams. You can feel yourself falling through the floor.

Before you know it, you're surrounded by water. The swirling waters begin to spin you around and around. A few feet away, you see a mattress floating near a large plank of wood. If you don't grab one of them, you'll surely drown.

To climb onto the mattress, turn to page 48.
To go for the wooden plank, turn to page 66.

Many homes in Johnstown were toppled from their foundations by the powerful flood and the large debris it carried.

You won't be separated from your father. You run to the front gate and into the street. The water is nearly up to your knees. You can't see your father among all the people, but you know he's somewhere up ahead.

You're nearly to the hill when you hear a deafening roar. You don't see the wave descend on you, but you feel its power sweep over you. You flail your arms about, but it's hopeless. You descend to a watery, but fortunately swift, death.

THE END

To follow another path, turn to page 9.
To learn more about the flood, turn to page 101.

The rushing water pushed the remains of crushed homes and uprooted trees many miles down the river.

You leap for the mattress. It dips into the water as you climb atop it, but it remains afloat. Everywhere you look there is water. You see roofs, walls, and whole buildings drifting by.

The current lifts the mattress and carries you downstream. As you move through the water, twigs and debris whip into your face and mouth. You spit them out and start to paddle with your hands. Maybe you can eventually reach land. It's your only hope.

You see you're not alone on this chaotic sea. People pass you by, floating on tree branches, broken porches, and other floating debris.

The roof of a house comes into sight with about 20 people standing on it. As it draws closer, you see a man with bright red hair pointing to you. He's speaking, but you can't hear his words.

The other people on the roof seem to be arguing with him about something. It looks like he wants to rescue you and take you aboard their raft. The roof draws nearer.

The red-haired man dives off the roof and swims toward you with swift, powerful strokes.

You're happy to see him approach . . . or are you? If he attempts to climb onto the mattress, you may both fall off. You grab a small board floating by. You could use it to warn him off. He's almost at the mattress.

To let him on the mattress, turn to page 50.
To stop him from getting aboard, turn to page 56.

The man reaches your mattress and pulls himself onto it. It sags a bit from the extra weight. You're so glad to see him that you throw your arms around his neck.

"It's okay," he says. "You're going to be all right." He tells you his name is Tom.

The roof with all the people on it is floating farther and farther away.

"Can we reach them?" you ask Tom.

"No, and even if we could it wouldn't matter," he says. "They told me that if I came back with you, they wouldn't let us get on. They're afraid the extra weight would sink the roof."

As the mattress floats downstream, you suddenly see a familiar landmark—the stone bridge where the trains cross the river. Everything swept up in the flood has collided with the bridge and dammed up the flood waters.

As you draw closer you can see the endless debris bottled up at the bridge. You see everything from trees and telephone poles to parts of houses and dead horses.

"We're going to run into the bridge," you say.

"There's a chance we can go around it," Tom replies. "See that narrow passageway that the water's going through? If we paddle in that direction, we can get through to the other side."

But what will you find on the other side? You point out that some people are moving across the mountain of debris on the bridge, trying to reach dry land.

"You're right," Tom says. "If we climb onto the bridge, maybe we can get safely across it to solid ground."

To steer for the bridge, turn to page 52.
To try to paddle around the bridge, turn to page 55.

Tom agrees that going for the bridge is your best bet. The two of you paddle toward the bridge, and the mattress hits one of the bridge's stone arches hard.

You scramble off the mattress and onto the arch. You cross over the roof of a barn and can smell the stench of dead horses. When you look down, you see a human hand poking out of a house window. You quickly turn away.

Soon you come upon bales of barbed wire. "We can't get through this," Tom says. "We'll have to find another way off the bridge."

Suddenly you smell something in the air, and it isn't dead horse flesh.

Tom's expression darkens as he also sniffs the air. "Oil," he says.

"Oil?" you repeat. "Where would that come from?"

"See all the freight train cars piled up around us?" Tom asks. "Maybe one of them was carrying oil and it's leaked out. It could spark a fire."

You shiver at the thought. "We need to get off this bridge, don't we?" you cry.

"We do," says Tom. "Let's find another way across it."

As you look around, you see a wrecked house. There is a door you can go through. Or you could climb up to what's left of the roof.

To go through the house, turn to page 54.
To go up and over the roof, turn to page 57.

You and Tom enter the house through the door. It's pitch dark inside. Tom holds your hand as you stumble through the darkness. You enter a second room and see something red and glowing.

"It looks like a coal stove that flipped over when the house was swept away," you say.

The coals are giving off a powerful heat. You think of the oil seeping through the debris and possibly this house as well. If the oil catches fire, it could spread and burn the bridge and everything on it.

"We'd better get out of here," you say.

Tom agrees. "Come on," he says, leading the way to the next room.

Turn to page 59.

The massive mountain of debris gives you second thoughts about going onto the bridge. Tom agrees that you could be trapped there and would be unable to get off.

You spy two wooden boards in the water. You grab them and hand one to Tom. You use the boards like oars to paddle toward the narrow opening. You manage to make it through and continue to float downriver.

Then you see it—a small boat with two men. They row the boat closer to your mattress. One of the men gestures to you. Your heart beats fast as you see him toss a rope into the air. It falls just short of reaching you. Tom paddles furiously toward the floating rope and tells you to lie flat so you can grab it.

Turn to page 68.

You lift the plank and swing it in the air.

"Don't come any nearer!" you cry out.

"Don't be foolish, girl," the man replies. "I've come to rescue you."

"Please, stay away!" you yell.

He doesn't listen and wrestles the board from you. As he does, you fall off the mattress and it drifts away.

"Now look what you've done!" he exclaims. "Our only hope now is to make it back to the roof."

Seeing you struggle in the water, he grabs you and pulls you along with him. Eventually you make it back to the roof, but the others aren't happy. The man has to argue with them to let you stay. You have indeed been a foolish girl!

THE END

To follow another path, turn to page 9.
To learn more about the flood, turn to page 101.

You and Tom scramble onto the roof. From here you can see the end of the bridge and the dry land beyond. You can also see the sky starting to darken. You'll have to hurry if you want to get off the bridge while it's still light.

You descend the other side of the roof and then walk across a tangle of trees. You follow Tom through the maze of debris to the stone arch and climb down from the bridge.

Turn the page.

Thousands of tons of debris were trapped against the Pennsylvania Railroad stone bridge that crossed the Little Conemaugh River.

ROOOSSH!

Suddenly you hear a sound like the swoosh of a great gust of wind. You turn and see a flash of light on the bridge.

"The fire," says Tom. "It's started."

You don't know what caused it, but you're glad you're off the bridge. You follow Tom toward the flattened streets of Johnstown.

You and Tom are surrounded by people. Some watch in horror as they hear the screams of people trapped on the burning bridge. You leave the bridge and head downtown. The streets are bare of buildings. It's as if Johnstown never existed.

You ask people you pass about your father, but barely anyone stops to answer. They're looking for their own family members and have no time for you.

Turn to page 60.

You follow Tom through to the rear door. He turns the doorknob, and it falls off in his hand. It was broken in the house's tumbled journey in the flood. Tom throws his weight against the damaged door, but it won't budge. He grabs a chair and smashes the window in the rear wall. But debris is heaped up on the other side, making it impossible to pass through.

"Quick!" cries Tom. "Run for the front door before the oil catches fire!"

You run for your life, with Tom following right behind you.

Turn to page 67.

Finally, a woman with a kind face stops as you speak to her. She doesn't know where your father is but wants to help.

"Come with me, girl," she says. "My house is still standing, and you can stay there tonight. We'll look for your father in the morning."

The woman means well, but you'd rather stay with Tom. If anyone can help find your father, it's him.

But Tom disagrees. "Maybe you should go with this lady," he says. "I've got my own family to find, you know."

> To stick with Tom, go to page 61.
> To go with the lady, turn to page 62.

"I want to stay with Tom," you tell the lady.

Tom looks up at the woman and smiles. She smiles back. She understands the situation.

"I hope you find your loved ones," she says before leaving.

You and Tom continue through the crowded streets.

Tom talks as you walk. He tells you how he was coming home from his job at the Cambria Iron Company when the flood waters struck. He joined the other people on the roof and was planning to look for his wife and son once they reached land.

"Then why did you leave the roof to rescue me?" you ask.

Turn to page 63.

You realize how much Tom wants to find his family. He can't worry about you anymore. You give him a hug, and he goes on his way.

The kind lady tells you her name is Mrs. Metz. She takes you to her house. It's one of only a few that still stands amid the rubble. After a change of clothes and a hot meal, you go to bed in a guest room. During the night, you toss restlessly in the small bed. But you eventually fall into a deep sleep.

Turn to page 65.

Tom gives a sad smile. "It's what I would've wanted another man to do if he found my wife and boy on the water," he says.

Suddenly, Tom stops and stares at a woman in a dirty, wet dress. Her pretty face is streaked with mud.

"Lily!" he cries, as she runs to his arms.

"Oh, my dear," Lily sobs. "I thought I'd never see you again."

"And I you," Tom replies, kissing his wife's face.

"Where's Willie?" he asks.

"I don't know," Lily says. "We were running from the house. I was holding his hand in mine, and then suddenly he was gone. I couldn't see him in the crowd. Then the big wave came . . .."

Turn the page.

Lily starts to cry uncontrollably, and Tom hugs her.

"We'll find him," he vows. "We've got to find him."

You hope Tom is right, but you can't stay with him. This is a private moment that you're not a part of. You begin to back away. The clinging couple don't notice you leaving. You must continue your own search for your father and sisters. You only hope your story has a happy ending.

THE END

To follow another path, turn to page 9.
To learn more about the flood, turn to page 101.

You wake up the next morning, wondering if all that's happened was a bad dream. You tiptoe downstairs to the front porch. On the sidewalk, you see a woman who looks oddly familiar.

You suddenly realize this is your Aunt Barbara, your father's sister. You cry out her name, and she turns to you. Her face turns pale, and her eyes grow wide. Before you can speak again, she flees down the street.

"Aunt Barbara!" you cry. But she's gone. You burst into tears. Didn't she recognize you?

Mrs. Metz comes out and asks what's wrong. You want to tell her what's happened, but your emotions overcome you.

Then you hear someone calling your name. You look up and see a man running toward you. Foam is coming out of his open mouth.

Turn to page 69.

You grab for the wooden board, but something sharp cuts your hand. It's a nail. You pull back in pain and lose your grip on the board. Now you're caught up in the swirling water. It's like a whirlpool, pulling you into its deadly center. You look around for something else to grab, but the mattress is too far away. The big question now is how long can you tread water?

THE END

To follow another path, turn to page 9.
To learn more about the flood, turn to page 101.

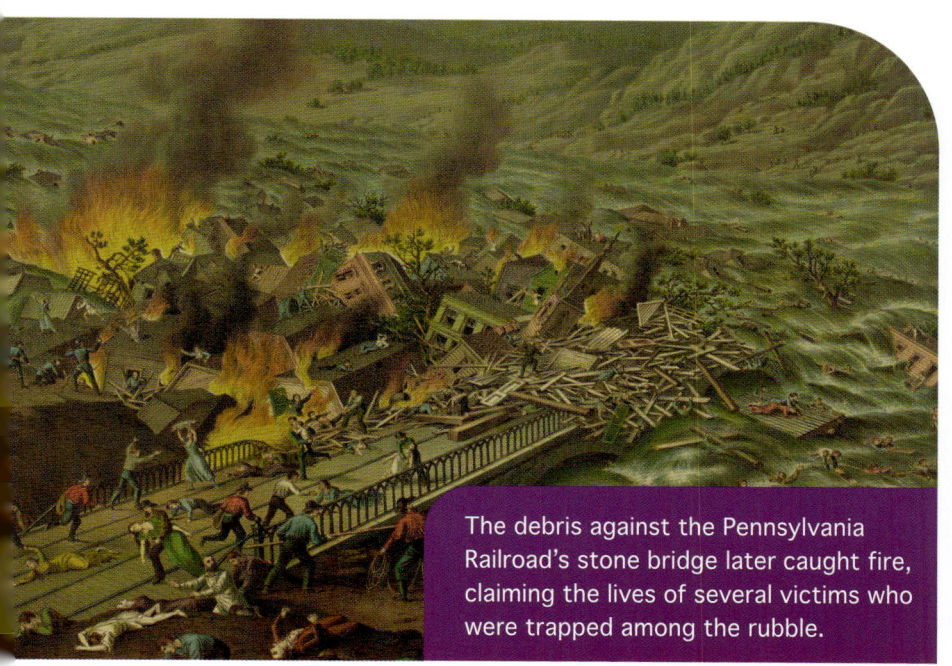

The debris against the Pennsylvania Railroad's stone bridge later caught fire, claiming the lives of several victims who were trapped among the rubble.

You race past the burning kitchen and out the front door. But the area surrounding the house is ablaze. "Jump into the water!" Tom cries. You do, but the water is covered with oil, too. Before you can swim away, the thick, oily smoke overcomes you. Dying by suffocation is no fun, but at least you won't burn to death.

THE END

To follow another path, turn to page 9.
To learn more about the flood, turn to page 101.

You lean out from the mattress and reach for the floating rope. As Tom gives a cheer, the men in the boat stop rowing. They haul in the rope and you with it. A large man grabs you in both arms. He smells of sweat and tobacco, but to you it smells as sweet as perfume. The other men help Tom into the boat.

The man holding you asks your name. He knows your father but can't tell you if he's among the survivors. You look back and see an eerie reddish glow in the sky.

"The bridge is burning," the man says. You and Tom made the right decision to steer away from it. You think of your family. Will you ever see them again? You'll find out soon enough. For now, you're just grateful to be alive.

THE END

To follow another path, turn to page 9.
To learn more about the flood, turn to page 101.

The man comes bounding up the porch and grabs you in his arms. You see now that the foam on his mouth is really shaving cream. It's your father!

"Your aunt ran to the house where we're staying up the street," he says in a voice hoarse with emotion. "I didn't believe her when she said she'd seen you. But here you are, alive!"

You introduce your father to Mrs. Metz. Then you follow him back to the house where he's staying with Aunt Barbara. You have a lot of catching up to do and adventures to share on this incredible day.

THE END

To follow another path, turn to page 9.
To learn more about the flood, turn to page 101.

In the late 1800s, the Cambria Iron Company was one of the largest producers of iron and steel in the United States.

CHAPTER 4
A CLERK TO THE RESCUE

It's 4:00 p.m. on a Friday afternoon at the Cambria Iron Company store. Although you're barely in your twenties, you're the managing clerk on duty. It's a holiday weekend, and with all the rain and street flooding, few people are venturing out. You're looking forward to closing the store within the hour. You want to go home to your family for the rest of this rainy weekend.

You're the third generation in your family to work for Cambria Iron. Your grandfather worked in the mills, and your father is a foreman there. The house you live in is a company house, which was built by Cambria. You're proud to be working for one of the biggest companies in central Pennsylvania.

Turn the page.

At 4:07 p.m. one of the clerks points out the window and cries, "Look!" You turn and see water rising quickly and rushing down the street.

How did the floodwaters get so high? you ask yourself. Then you realize this can't just be rainwater causing the river to flood. *It must be the South Fork Dam . . . it's burst!*

When the South Fork dam collapsed at Lake Conemaugh, it released billions of gallons of water that rushed down the river valley, destroying everything in its path.

You cry out a warning to the other clerks. "We've got to get upstairs before the floor is flooded!"

Then you lead the way to the staircase. There isn't a moment to spare.

You're halfway up the staircase when you stop. There's no time to salvage goods on the first floor, but there's something that should be saved. In the manager's office is a tin box with $12,000 cash. It might be lost if the waters flood the office. As a good company man, you should go back for it. But is there time?

To go back for the money box, turn to page 74.
To keep running for your life, turn to page 76.

With only moments to spare, you rush back downstairs and into the office. You sweep the tin box up in one arm and rush up the staircase. At the top of the stairs, you see the other clerks standing in a semicircle. They're waiting for you to tell them what to do next. The water is rising quickly. It's already almost ankle-deep.

It doesn't take long for the water to rise up to your knees. It's ice cold and numbs your thoughts. There's a lot of merchandise on the second floor, including samples of steel rails and other company products.

It's time you headed for the third floor, but should you try to take some of these things with you? None of it is as valuable as the $12,000 in the tin box under your arm.

The Cambria Iron Company's factory buildings suffered heavy damage in the flood.

As you try to decide what to do, you feel a chill in your legs. You look down and see the water is now up to your waist.

"What do we do?" Sam, the youngest clerk, asks you.

To take merchandise to the third floor, turn to page 77.

To forget the goods and head directly upstairs, turn to page 79.

Your life is worth more than the money in the box, you tell yourself. You start up the stairs behind the others. The water is like a living thing, chasing you up the staircase, step by step. You panic and slip. You hit your head on the edge of a step and are knocked out.

A minute later you come to and rise to your feet, but the water is all around you, and you stumble again. You cry for help, but the other clerks can't hear you over the noise of the rushing waters. You splash around in the water that grows deeper every moment. It's a pity you never learned to swim.

THE END

To follow another path, turn to page 9.
To learn more about the flood, turn to page 101.

Your life may be in danger, but you're still loyal to the company. "Let's get whatever we can carry to the third floor," you tell the others.

Each of them lifts a piece of merchandise and carries it up the stairs. Sam is struggling to lift a sack of goods. "You go on, Sam," you say, grabbing the sack. "I'll handle this one."

You hoist up the heavy sack and lug it upstairs. When you put it down, you look around to count the clerks. Five . . . six . . . seven . . . wait, someone's missing. It's Sam!

You rush over to the railing. Bounding up the stairs comes Sam, holding the tin box with the money. There is a triumphant grin on his face. You can't believe you forgot about the box after putting it down to help Sam.

Turn the page.

After the flood, much of Johnstown was destroyed and the streets were choked with rubble and debris.

"Good work, Sam!" you cry, clapping him on the back.

He smiles back at you, pleased by your praise.

You head up to the third floor. You'll be safe there, but for how long? Looking over the railing, you see a small lake of churning waves below. The waters aren't receding, but they aren't getting higher either.

You turn your attention to the food stored on the third floor. You can smell freshly baked loaves of bread, sides of bacon, beef, and hunks of ham. Some of the meat is cooked and some raw. You can hear your stomach rumble and recall that you haven't eaten since breakfast.

You look out a window and see houses floating by in the distance. People are clinging to some of them.

Turn the page.

When you lean further out the window, you can see that only a few buildings are still standing. The Cambria Iron Company store is one of them. This puts you in a unique position to rescue other people. You tell this to your fellow clerks, and they're all eager to help.

"But let's eat something first to keep our strength up," says a stout clerk named Derek.

You'd love to stop and eat something. But rescuing people from the flood is the first priority. Most of the other clerks, however, agree with Derek that you should eat first.

To rescue other people first, go to page 81.

To eat first and then start the rescue effort, turn to page 84.

"We can eat later," you say to the others.

"But we need food first," Derek says. "Let's put it to a vote."

A vote might mean you'll lose. So you quickly think up a compromise.

"How about this . . . two men can eat at a time while the others work on rescue efforts," you explain. "This way everyone can take a turn at eating."

Derek doesn't seem sold on your compromise, but everyone else is. Two clerks are chosen to be the first to eat. Then the rest of you move to the windows.

Turn the page.

You look out the window and see a man clinging to a log. You wave to him, and he begins paddling wildly with his hands. He lunges for the windowsill and just reaches it.

You can try to pull him in yourself or call the others over to help. Working as a rescue team might be better, but is there time?

To get help, go to page 83.
To rescue the man yourself, turn to page 96.

People caught in the floodwaters clung desperately to floating logs, pieces of wood, and anything else they could find.

"Quick!" you cry to the others. "I need help!"

You tell them to link their arms and join you at the window. Holding on to the clerk next to you, you lean forward, grab the man's hand, and pull him up. With the chain of men behind you helping, you're able to lift him up and through the window. He falls to the floor with a thud. He looks up at you with grateful eyes. "You just saved my life!" he gasps.

You grin and the others give a cheer. You've saved one life from the flood. Can you save others? You're eager to try.

Turn to page 85.

The clerks are hungry and eager to eat. You have them pull out a long table and set down plates and silverware from the kitchen. You find a cooked side of roast beef.

It smells a little funky but not too bad. You eat a few slices. A short time later your stomach is feeling queasy. Then you start sweating. Several other clerks who ate the beef are showing similar symptoms. You feel the need to lie down and rest.

Turn to page 97.

You return to the window to look for more people to save. But you see no one. You glance back at the tin box behind you on the floor. In the coming hours, there may be more rescued people joining you on the third floor. You don't want to think that any of them would steal the money, but you don't want to tempt anyone. You could have the clerks take turns guarding the box or you could take the responsibility on yourself.

> To ask Sam to watch the money box, turn to page 86.
>
> To ask Derek to guard the money, turn to page 87.
>
> To protect the money box yourself, turn to page 89.

Sam showed real initiative when he retrieved the money box. You ask him to take the first shift of guarding it. He's delighted to have this honor. To keep him busy as he sits guard, you have him cut up pieces of canvas. Then you tell him to wrap pieces of the meat and bread in them. This food can be given to rescued people.

One of the other clerks comes to you with coils of heavy rope he's found in a closet. "We can use the rope as a lifeline to throw out to people in the flood," he says.

"Good idea," you reply, but then you think of another use for the rope. You've noticed a lot of wooden boards and planks floating by. You could use the rope to snag the boards and bring them inside. Then you could tie them together and make a raft to save more people.

To use the rope to rescue people, turn to page 88.
To use the rope to make a raft, turn to page 90.

You ask Derek to take the first shift of guarding the money box. Although the two of you aren't the best of friends, you feel you can trust him.

Derek accepts the job eagerly and you go back to the window. A woman clinging to the limb of a tree suddenly comes into sight. The limb brushes up against the window. You and another clerk grab her and pull her into the building.

While someone wraps a blanket around the drenched woman, you turn and see Derek staring into the opened money box. He may not be as trustworthy as you thought. Should you take the box from him or find a better way to handle the situation?

To take the box from Derek, turn to page 92.
To give Derek a different task, turn to page 93.

You take one length of rope and tie a loop around one end. Soon a man floats into view, and you toss the rope out the window toward him. He grabs the end and holds on for dear life.

You call to another clerk to help you haul the man to safety. You pull hard on the rope. It's a challenging task because you're struggling against the pull of the water. You tug on the rope with every muscle. The man draws closer and closer to the window.

Turn to page 94.

You feel that the only person you can trust with the money is yourself. You put it down at your feet and notice that the box's latch is loose.

As you lift the latch to examine it, a gust of wind roars through the window. Half the paper bills in the box go fluttering through the air. They float down the steps and into the water below. Maybe when the water recedes, you'll be able to get the money back. Or maybe not. You've made a stupid mistake. And now everyone in the room knows it.

THE END

To follow another path, turn to page 9.
To learn more about the flood, turn to page 101.

You make a small loop at the end of one piece of rope and toss it toward a passing plank. You miss and try again. It takes a while, but you soon master the art of snagging planks and pulling them in.

Several people bravely risked their own lives to try to save others from the deadly flood.

Once you have enough wood, you have the men tie them together with some rope. The next step is to tie the remaining ropes at each end to posts anchored to the floor and to the raft. Now comes the final test for your rescue raft.

You and three other clerks carry the raft to the window. It just fits through. Then you ease it down into the flood waters. The raft bobs and twists this way and that in the churning waves. But the ropes hold!

Soon a young girl floats into sight and grabs the side of the raft. Then a man appears. He pulls himself up onto the raft and helps the girl aboard. A third person climbs on. And a fourth. You and the other clerks give a cheer. Now comes the hard part—pulling them in to safety. Several of you grab the ropes and pull with all your strength.

Turn to page 99.

Derek looks at you with shifty eyes.

"You're not supposed to open the box," you say.

"I was just seeing how much money there is," he replies.

You don't buy his excuse. "Hand over the box, Derek," you demand.

His eyes flash with anger. "So, you don't trust me, do you?" he says.

"I did trust you, but now I see my trust was misplaced," you say. "Now hand it over."

Instead, Derek swings out with his right fist, just missing your jaw. Then he lowers his head and rams into your stomach, knocking you to the floor.

Turn to page 95.

"You don't have to count the money," you tell Derek. "I know how much is there."

Derek's eyes narrow. Guilt is written all over his face.

"Sure," he gulps. "I just thought I'd—"

"It's okay," you say. "Actually, I was thinking that with your muscles, you should be at the window helping to rescue people."

Derek doesn't argue with you. He almost seems relieved when he hands you the money box. It's as if he's grateful that you removed the temptation to steal the money. He's a hard fellow to figure out, but you think you handled this delicate situation the best way.

Turn to page 98.

The man is only a few feet from the window when you see the rope is coming apart. The tension of the water and the weight of the man is too much for it. You pull the rope faster and faster. It's a race against time. He's almost within reach when the rope snaps. You see the surprised expression on the man's face as he's swept away by the rushing waters.

You pull the end of the rope in and crumple to the floor with your head in your hands. You'll never forget the look on the man's face. It will stay with you for the rest of your life.

THE END

To follow another path, turn to page 9.
To learn more about the flood, turn to page 101.

You leap to your feet and deliver a blow to Derek's belly. He goes down like a sack of flour. Two other clerks grab Derek.

"What shall we do with him?" they ask you.

"Tie him up with some rope and let him cool off," you tell them.

From now on, you'll keep the money box to yourself. You return to the window just in time to see a clerk lift a small boy from the water. The woman you rescued earlier gives a cry. "My son!" she exclaims.

The child is cold and shivering but very much alive. You hand him to his mother. You and your men are true heroes on a day when heroes are desperately needed. Congratulations!

THE END

To follow another path, turn to page 9.
To learn more about the flood, turn to page 101.

You fear if you wait for the others to join you, the man will lose his grip on the window and be swept away. You thrust out your arm and clasp his hand. But he weighs more than you. Instead of you pulling him into the building, he pulls you out into the flood waters.

Now you are both clinging to that same log. But the chance of finding another building still standing with people to rescue you is extremely slim. Your future looks pretty grim!

THE END

To follow another path, turn to page 9.
To learn more about the flood, turn to page 101.

As time passes the pain in your stomach grows worse. You and the others who ate the bad beef take turns going to the window to throw up. You'll feel better in a few hours, but by then the flood waters will be receding. Any hopes you had of being heroes will be over. Too bad you didn't eat the cooked ham instead.

THE END

To follow another path, turn to page 9.
To learn more about the flood, turn to page 101.

Derek wastes no time in his new job as rescuer. He soon pulls a child from the flood through the window. "My dog! My dog!" cries the boy.

You look out and see a German shepherd clinging to a tree trunk several yards away. The dog sees you and swims toward you. He makes it within several feet of the building. But he looks out of strength and about to be swept away.

"Grab my legs," Derek tells you. He leans out of the window and you grab his legs as he grabs the dog. The boy cries as he rushes to hug his pet.

You slap Derek on the back. The man you took for a thief has turned out to be a hero.

THE END

To follow another path, turn to page 9.
To learn more about the flood, turn to page 101.

Inch by painful inch, you and your crew pull in the raft. After several minutes, the raft is alongside the window. One by one, you lift the people off the raft and into the building.

The clerks give them towels to dry off and blankets to keep warm. Meanwhile, you let out the raft again to rescue more victims. By morning, you have rescued 19 people from the flood, including six children.

Some people are more difficult to reach. They're sitting on rooftops or other secure places. You send out food wrapped in canvas on the raft to them. You feed nearly 100 people this way. As a new day breaks, the devastation is shocking. But you and your team have saved lives and are true heroes of the Johnstown Flood.

THE END

To follow another path, turn to page 9.
To learn more about the flood, turn to page 101.

A view from a hill, overlooking the destruction of Johnstown after the flood

CHAPTER 5
A TRAGEDY'S LONG SHADOW

The Johnstown Flood was a disaster of epic proportions. The official death toll was 2,209, including 99 entire families with 396 children.

One out of 10 people living in Johnstown died in the flood. About 750 victims were so disfigured by the water and fires that they could not be identified. They were buried in what came to be called the Unknown Plot in Johnstown's Grandview Cemetery.

Many bodies were carried many miles away by the raging waters. The last body to be found was in Cincinnati, Ohio. It was recovered in 1911—22 years after the flood.

About 1,600 homes were destroyed and 4 square miles (10 square km) of downtown Johnstown was leveled to the ground. The loss in property damage totaled $17 million. In 2021 dollars that would be more than $493 million.

Two of the stories in this book are based on the experiences of actual survivors.

"The Girl on the Mattress" is based loosely on Gertrude Quinn. She was only six years old at the time. The real Gertrude was rescued by a mill worker named Maxwell McAchren. He threw Gertrude across 15 feet (4.6 m) of water into the arms of a man in a nearby building.

The hero of "A Clerk to the Rescue" is based on Thomas Magee, a clerk at the Cambria Iron Company store. He actually saved $12,000 from the store. With courage and inventiveness, Magee's team rescued 19 people from the third story of the store using a handmade raft.

The newlywed couple in "A Honeymoon Interrupted" weren't real people. But their challenges getting to higher ground were based on the experiences of surviving train passengers in East Conemaugh.

Many journalists covering the flood accused the South Fork Fishing and Hunting Club of negligence. They said the club was responsible for the dam failure and the resulting tragedy.

Some club members, including Andrew Carnegie, gave generously to the Johnstown relief fund. However, none admitted any responsibility.

A few survivors brought lawsuits against the club, but they were not successful. The club was disbanded soon after. The dam and the lake it created were never rebuilt.

The Red Cross provided food and shelter to the survivors of the Johnstown Flood.

Clara Barton was founder and president of the American Red Cross beginning in 1881.

There were several heroes during the aftermath of the Johnstown Flood. Chief among them was 67-year-old Clara Barton, founder of the American Red Cross. Barton's team stayed for five months to help heal and comfort the injured and homeless. After the Johnstown Flood, the Red Cross was seen as the most important relief organization in the nation.

The Johnstown Flood became one of the biggest events since the end of the Civil War. The flood inspired books, songs, memorials, and dramatic recreations. In 1990, the film *The Johnstown Flood* won an Academy Award for Best Documentary, Short Subject.

The Johnstown Flood is a compelling story of the destruction that hit the unsuspecting townspeople on a rainy Friday afternoon in May 1889. It lives on in the minds and hearts of Americans to this day.

JOHNSTOWN FLOOD TIMELINE

1830S—
The State of Pennsylvania completes an earth-filled dam across the Conemaugh River to create a lake reservoir for a rail and canal system between Philadelphia and Pittsburgh.

1857—
The dam and water system are bought by the Pennsylvania Railroad.

1879—
Benjamin Ruff develops the property into an exclusive summer resort, the South Fork Fishing and Hunting Club. The club rebuilds the old dam to create Lake Conemaugh for recreational use.

1885, 1887, 1888—
Johnstown, 14 miles (23 km) downriver from the dam, experiences heavy flooding from spring rains.

MAY 30, 1889—
Heavy rains come down on the region by late afternoon and continue overnight.

3:10 P.M., MAY 31, 1889—
The neglected and deteriorating South Fork dam, overwhelmed by rising rainwater, bursts.

4:07 P.M., MAY 31, 1889—
The flood waters reach Johnstown, causing widespread death and destruction.

JUNE 5, 1889—
Clara Barton, founder of the American Red Cross, arrives in Johnstown with a team of doctors and nurses to help in the aftermath of the flood.

1911—
The remains of the last flood victim is recovered in Cincinnati, Ohio, about 400 miles (644 km) from Johnstown.

OTHER PATHS TO EXPLORE

In this book, you've seen how events from the past look different from three points of view. Perspectives on history are as varied as the people who lived it. Seeing history from many points of view is an important part of understanding it. Here are some other Johnstown Flood points of view to explore:

>>> The wealthy members of the South Fork Fishing and Hunting Club did not accept any blame for the breaking dam and the terrible flood that resulted from it. Why do you think they weren't held accountable by the law? If this tragic event happened today, do you think the situation would be different? Why or why not? What current events can you look at as a comparison?

>>> Part of the reason so many people died in the Johnstown Flood is that they had little or no warning. This was also true for other natural disasters in early U.S. History, such as earthquakes, fires, and hurricanes. How does new technology change that? How is the loss of life reduced when these disasters happen today? Support your answer with examples.

BIBLIOGRAPHY

McCullough, David. *The Johnstown Flood*. New York: Simon & Schuster, 1968.

Roker, Al. *Ruthless Tide: The Heroes and Villains of the Johnstown Flood*. New York: HarperCollins, 2018.

"Run For Your Lives!" by David McCullough, *American Heritage*, June 1966, pp. 4-11, 66-75.

Wallechinsky, David and Irving Wallace. "The Johnstown Flood," *The People's Almanac*. Garden City, NY: Doubleday, 1975.

GLOSSARY

canal (kuh-NAL)—a channel that is dug across land; canals connect bodies of water so ships can travel between them

compromise (KAHM-pruh-myz)—an agreement in which each side gives up something they want to make a deal

crest (KREST)—the highest point of something, such as the top of a hill or a wave

engineer (en-juh-NEER)—someone trained to design and build machines and structures; also, someone who operates a train

engulf (en-GUHLF)—to flow over or overwhelm something

foreman (FAWR-muhn)—a person in charge of a group of workers

heirloom (AIR-loom)—a valuable object that belongs to a family and is handed down from generation to generation

negligence (NEH-glih-juhns)—failure to properly care for something

recede (rih-SEED)—to move back and away from a previous position

reservoir (REH-zuhr-vwahr)—an artificial lake where water is collected

READ MORE

Cummings, Judy Dodge. *Earth, Wind, Fire, and Rain: Real Tales of Temperamental Elements*. White River Junction, VT: Nomad Press, 2018.

Huddleston, Emma. *The Johnstown Flood*. Minneapolis: Abdo Publishing, 2020.

Richards, Marlee. *The Johnstown Flood: Core Events of a Deadly Disaster*. North Mankato, MN: Capstone Press, 2014.

INTERNET SITES

Facts About the 1889 Flood
jaha.org/attractions/johnstown-flood-museum/flood-history/facts-about-the-1889-flood/

How America's Most Powerful Men Caused America's Deadliest Flood
history.com/news/how-americas-most-powerful-men-caused-americas-deadliest-flood

Johnstown Flood National Memorial Pennsylvania
nps.gov/jofl/index.htm

ABOUT THE AUTHOR

Steven Otfinoski has written more than 200 books for young readers. Among his many books for Capstone are *Day of Infamy: The Story of the Attack on Pearl Harbor*, *Japanese American Internment: Prisoners in Their Own Land* and *The Selma Marches for Civil Rights: We Shall Overcome*. Three of his nonfiction books have been named Books for the Teen Age by the New York Public Library. He lives in Connecticut with his wife and two dogs.

Photo Credits
Alamy: Beryl Peters Collection, 12, BG/OLOU, 29, Chronicle, 24, Niday Picture Library, 6, 20, 31, 82, 90, Science History Images, 40; Getty Images: Stock Montage, 47; Library of Congress, Cover, 78, bottom 104, Histed, Ernest Walter, 70, 75, top 104; Newscom: Everett Collection, 45, 57; Shutterstock: Ev. Safronov, (water) Cover, design element throughout, Everett Collection, 67, 72, 100